5-Ingredient Keto Desserts

54 Fat-Burning Ketogenic Desserts (Sweets, Cookies, Ice-Creams, Fat Bombs And More)

RONNIE ISRAEL

ISBN-13:978-1727339260

ISBN-10:1727339266

DEDICATION

For Rosie,

Pleasant memories, always!

TABLE OF CONTENTS

Other Books By Ronnie Israel

The Keto Bread Cookbook: Top Low-Carb Ketogenic Bread Recipes For Weight Loss And Optimum Health

Quick Keto Meals: Easy Ketogenic Cooking In 30 Minutes Or Less

One Pot Keto: Easy Ketogenic Meals For Your Slow Cooker, Skillet, Stockpot And More

Electric Pressure Cooker Recipes: Over 100 Delicious Quick And Easy Recipes For Fast Meals

The Wok Cookbook: Delicious And Filling Chinese Recipes To Enjoy

INTRODUCTION

No kidding! Desserts make us happy! Just one bite of our favorite sweet treat can instantly transport us to a land of bliss and thrills, where nothing else matters but the sweetness in our palate. At that moment, we are happier; we are in a better mood and we feel good. If approached properly, desserts can enhance our emotional and physical wellness in numerous ways. Emotional, because of the way they make us feel; physical, because they can be healthy.

Then there is the ketogenic diet. This is a very popular diet that has drawn the attention of a large number or people on account of its tremendous health benefits. It promotes weight loss, reduces inflammation, reverse diabetes, counter obesity, prevent neurodegenerative diseases, battle cancer and lower blood pressure. In short, it is a highly effective diet that addresses many illnesses and diseases that people regularly face. High in fat and low in carbohydrates, the keto diet do not allow as many sugars or carbs. This means you may have do to without some of your favorite desserts. Interestingly, this is why many people shy away from dieting. They associate dieting with eating bland, distasteful means in a bid to keep fit and healthy. But they are wrong!

As important as it is to eat right and stay on keto track, everyone deserves a bit of indulgence and special treat. And if you have a sweet tooth, you can reward yourself with a keto dessert that will not deter you from your ketosis goal and still taste just as good and satisfying as traditional desserts. As a matter of fact, the amount of carbs and sugar in a dessert does not really determine its sweetness.

Additionally, the beauty of the keto diet is the availability of ketogenic substitutes for almost every traditional meal, desserts inclusive. For instance, there are great keto sweeteners like erythritol, xylitol, monk fruit and stevia available for use. So while you cannot have sugar, you can still enjoy sweet desserts ranging from cakes, cookies, candies, cheesecakes, muffin to ice creams and other frozen desserts. You won't feel like you are missing out on anything by the time you get down to it.

Remember also that desserts can be healthy. Desserts that contain keto-friendly fruits like strawberries and raspberries can be included in a dessert recipe to produce the expected results. We are also able to fulfill our daily fruit requirements easily.

This cookbook contains tasty and indulgent recipes that don't take hours in the kitchen to make. With just 5 ingredients or less, you can have your sweet treat ready in a few minutes. You do not need to worry about going out of ketosis anytime soon. I can guarantee this: you will absolutely enjoy it!

Ronnie Israel

CANDIES AND CONFECTIONS

Salted Toffee Walnut Cups

Prep Time: 20 minutes

Cook Time: 5 minutes

Servings: 5

Ingredients

5 oz milk chocolate, low-carb

5 tablespoons erythritol, divided

3 tablespoons cold butter

½ oz raw walnuts, chopped

Salt to taste

Preparation

1. Place the chocolate in the microwave and melt at 45- second intervals with frequent stirring.

2. Line a cupcake pan with 5 paper liners and spoon a chocolate into each liner. Spread to cover the bottom evenly and then use a pastry brush or spoon to brush up the chocolate edges a little. Freeze to harden.

3. Combine the erythritol and cold butter in a microwave bowl and heat for 3 minutes, stirring every 30 seconds or so to prevent burning. If mixture is too watery afterwards, thicken with extra 2 teaspoons of erythritol and add the chopped walnuts as well.

4. Take out the chocolate cups from the freezer and if necessary, reheat. Now fill each cup with a spoon of the toffee mixture. Stir slowly and work quickly because the mixture will begin to separate and harden.

5. Top with the rest of the chocolate and refrigerate an hour to cool.

6. Take them out from cups and then sprinkle with salt.

Nutritional info per serving

Calories 194.4; carbs: 2.5g; fats: 18.76 g; protein: 2.5g

Almond Coconut Bonbons

Who can resist a creamy coconut bonbon that's stuffed with almonds & chocolate chips?

Prep Time: 10minutes

Cook Time: 20minutes

Servings: 13

Ingredients

2/3 cup of sweetened condensed milk

1 cup unsweetened coconut, finely shredded

½ cup of almonds, sliced

1 cup sweetened chocolate chips, divided

 2 teaspoons of coconut oil

Preparation

1. Combine the condensed milk, almonds, ¼ cup of chocolate chips as well as coconut together.

2. Form into balls and place on a lined baking sheet. Freeze for 20 minutes.

3. Add chocolate chips and coconut oil to a microwave-bowl and melt.

4. Dip frozen bonbons into the melted chocolate and place back in the freezer to harden.

5. Refrigerate afterwards.

Nutritional info per serving

Calories 198; carbs: 7g; fats: 18g; protein: 3g

Salty Seedy Chocolate
A perfect mix of sweet and salty

Prep Time: 5 minutes

Cook Time: 5 minutes

Servings: 10

Ingredients

3 ounce of 90% dark chocolate

Dash of stevia or erythritol

1/4 cup of roasted pumpkin seeds

1/2 tablespoon of sea salt

Preparation

1. Melt the dark chocolate and sweetener in a microwave and stir. Melt again for about 30 seconds until thoroughly melted.

2. Combine most of the roasted pumpkin seeds with the thoroughly melted chocolate, reserving a small portion for sprinkling.

3. Line a baking pan with parchment paper and pour the mixture into it. Smooth the top with a spatula.

4. Sprinkle the sea salt and the reserved toasted pumpkin seeds on top. Refrigerate for 10-15 minutes to set.

5. Cut and enjoy the chocolates.

Nutritional info per serving

Calories 37; carbs: 5g; fats: 3g; protein:1g

Yogurt Berry Popsicles

Your summer won't be complete without this decadent treat.

Prep time: 5 minutes

Cook time: 0 minutes

Servings: 20

Ingredients:

1 pound of strawberries

2 cups of plain yogurt or kefir

¼ cup of sweetener

Preparation

1. Blend all the ingredients together until smooth.

2. Pour the mixture into Popsicle molds and freeze until they set.

Nutritional Info Per Serving

Calories: 22, Carbs: 2g, Fat: 0g, Proteins:1g

Sugar-Free Peanut Butter Fudge

A fantastic guilt-free recipe!

Preparation time: 5 minutes

Cooking time: 0 minutes

Servings: 12

Ingredients:

1 cup of coconut oil

1 cup of unsweetened peanut butter

1/4 cup of unsweetened vanilla almond milk

2 teaspoons vanilla liquid stevia, optional

A pinch of salt, optional

<u>**Preparation**</u>

1. Melt the coconut oil and peanut butter a little in a microwave.

2. Put in your blender along with the other ingredient and blend until it is well mixed.

3. Line a loaf pan with parchment paper and pour the mixture into it.

4. Keep in refrigerator for about 2 hours until it sets.

Nutritional Info Per Serving

Calories - 287, Carbs - 4g, Fat - 29.7g, Proteins - 5.4g

Keto Milk Chocolate

Prep Time: 10 minutes

Cook Time 20 minutes

Servings: 13

Ingredients

5ounce of cocoa butter

5ounce of baking chocolate, unsweetened, chopped

21/2 ounce of powdered erythritol

1ounce of whey protein powder

 3/4 teaspoon of liquid stevia extract

Preparation

1. Add together the whey protein and erythritol, blending well to combine to fine powder.

2. Melt the cocoa butter, with continuous stirring, in a double boiler or a small pan over low heat.

3. Add the baking chocolate and keep stirring until smooth.

4. Now add the whey protein and erythritol as well as the stevia, while stirring to mix well.

5. Remove from heat and stir to smoothness.

6. Pour into chocolate molds and place in the refrigerator to cool and hardened.

7. Enjoy at room temperature.

(Note that the nutrition info below does not include erythritol because the body cannot digest it).

Nutritional info per serving

Calories 170; carbs: 3.5 g; fats: 16g; protein: 3g

Dark Choc Caramels

Sinfully decadent!

Prep Time: 25 minutes

Cook Time: 0 minutes

Servings: 24

Ingredients:

2 cups of pitted medjool dates

1 1/2 cups of sunflower seeds, unsalted, roasted

3/4 cup of chocolate chips, nondairy

1/4 teaspoon of fine sea salt

Preparation

1. Blend in a food processor, the fine sea salt, dates and sunflower seeds until it forms a thick batter.

2. Put the batter into an 8x8-inch baking pan and press down firmly. Freeze pan for 20 minutes at least.

3. In the mean time, melt the chocolate chips.

4. Take out the frozen pan and loosen edges with a butter knife. Line a cutting board with parchment paper and then turn the pan over the board and divide the date mixture into small pieces.

5. Now drizzle a small dollop of chocolate on each piece. Get the melted chocolate along its edges and also smooth it out with the spoon's back.

6. Sprinkle the sea salt over it and refrigerate for 20 minutes to harden the chocolate.

Nutrition Per Serving

Calories: 60, Fat: 2.9g, Carbs: 8.4g, Protein: 1.2g

BARS

Chocolate Cheesecake Bars

Prep Time: 10 minutes

Cook Time: 30 minutes

Servings: 16

Ingredients

1 18-ounce roll chocolate chip cookie dough, refrigerated

1 cup softened cream cheese

1/2 cup of granulated sugar

1/2 teaspoon of vanilla extract

1 egg room temperature

Preparation

1. Preheat your oven to 350°F.

2. Spread ¾ of the cookie dough onto the bottom of a lined baking dish and press firmly down to create an even layer.

3. Beat the cream cheese with a mixer until fluffy. Add the sugar and whisk to combine well. Add in the egg and vanilla extract, beating until smooth.

4. Pour cheesecake filling over cookie dough base. Break the rest of the cookie dough and crumble over as well.

5. Bake for about 30 minutes. Cool, cut into bars and refrigerate in a container.

Nutritional info per serving

Calories 128; carbs: 14g; fats: 8g; protein: 2g

Bounty Bar Chocolate Bark

A soft and creamy dark chocolate

Prep Time: 25 minutes

Cook Time: minutes

Servings: 15

Ingredients

7 oz dark chocolate

1 cup unsweetened desiccated coconut

3 tablespoons of coconut cream

1 tablespoon of coconut oil

1 to 2 tablespoons of granulated sweetener

Liquid stevia, optional

Preparation

1. Melt half of the chocolate and sweeten with drops of stevia, if using.

2. Pour the chocolate into a lined casserole dish and spread evenly. Harden in the refrigerator.

3. In a food processor, combine the desiccated coconut, coconut cream, oil and sweetener.

4. Spread the mixture over the hardened chocolate base and then press firmly down.

5. Now melt the reserved half of the chocolate and pour melted chocolate over the top.

6. Finally. Sprinkle with some coconut and place in the refrigerator until set.

Nutritional info per serving

Calories 106; carbs: 1.2g; fats: 9.7g; protein: 2.2g

Cashew Lemon Bars

Prep Time: 5minutes

Freeze Time: 3 hours

Servings: 6

Ingredients

1 cup of cashews

3 tablespoons lemon juice

3/4 cup coconut cream

1 tablespoon of raw honey

1 Vanilla Shortbread Collagen Protein Bar

2 teaspoons of lemon zest

Preparation

1. 3 hours before cooking, soak the cashews in water.

2. Now add the soaked cashews, together with the lemon juice and coconut cream to a food processor and pulse about 3 minutes until smooth.

3. Add the honey and pulse again for 30 seconds.

4. Pour the mixer into 6 cupcake tins and top with crumbled collagen bar and lemon zest.

5. Freeze for 3 hours

Nutritional info per serving

Calories 243; carbs: 11.5g; fats: 19.3g; protein: 6.3g

COOKIES

No-Bake Keto Cookies

Satisfy your sweet tooth with these creamy and crunchy cookies.

Prep Time: 5 minutes

Cook Time 5 minutes

Servings: 18

Ingredients

2 tablespoons of real butter

2/3 cup of peanut butter

1 cup of unsweetened coconut, shredded

4 drops of vanilla stevia

Preparation

1. Add butter to microwave bowl, place in the microwave and melt.

2. Add peanut butter, stir, and add the sweetener as well as the coconut, mixing well.

3. Transfer to sheet pan and freeze for 5 to 10 minutes.

4. Bag and refrigerate, afterwards.

Nutritional info per serving

Calories 80; carbs: 0g; fats: 0g; protein: 0g

Chewy Chocolate Cookies

Moist, chewy, decadent cookies!

Prep Time: 10 minutes

Cook Time: 12 minutes

Servings: 15

Ingredients

1 1/2 cups of almond butter

2 eggs

1/2 cup natural sweetener

1/3 cup unsweetened and sifted cocoa powder

1 teaspoon vanilla extract, sugar-free

1 pinch salt

Preparation

1. Preheat your oven to 350°F.

2. In a food processor, add the eggs, butter, cocoa powder, sweetener, salt and vanilla extract and pulse until the mixture becomes dough.

3. Roll the dough into small balls and place on a baking sheet that is lined with parchment paper. Use a fork to press down twice in a crisscross pattern.

3. Bake about 12 minutes in the preheated oven and remove once edges are firm.

4. Cool 1 minute on the baking sheet and then transfer to a wire rack to cool very well.

Nutritional info per serving

Calories 173; carbs: 12.9g; fats: 15.7g; protein: 5g

Easy Peanut Butter Cookies

Prep Time: 10minutes

Cook Time: 10minutes

Servings: 15 cookies

Ingredients

1 cup peanut butter, no-added sugar

1 large egg

1/2 cup granular erythritol

Preparation

1. Preheat oven to 350°F.

2. Blend the granular erythritol into a fine powder and then combine with the egg, mixing well.

3. Roll dough into balls and place on a baking sheet that has been lined with parchment paper. Use a fork to press down the balls twice so that a cookie pattern can be created on the peanut butter.

4. Bake 10 to 15 minutes until cookie turns darker brown along the edges.

5. Cool on a wire rack and serve with a glass of low carb nut milk.

Nutritional info per serving

Calories 105; carbs: 2g; fats: 9g; protein: 4g

Lemon Almond Shortbread Cookies

Enjoy the perfect keto shortbread cookies!

Prep Time: 30minutes

Cook Time: 15minutes

Servings: 18 cookies

Ingredients

6 tablespoons of butter

2 cups of almond flour

1/3 cup granulated sweetener

1 teaspoon of lemon zest, freshly grated

Preparation

1. Melt butter and then add the almond flour, lemon zest and sweetener, mixing well to combine until crumbly.

2. Form into a cylinder and then compress dough by wrapping tightly with a plastic wrap.

3. Freeze 30 minutes or refrigerate 2 hours until firm enough to slice well.

4. Slice into cookies of ½ inch thickness.

5. Line a cookie sheet with parchment paper and bake in a preheated oven for 15 minutes at 350°F until golden brown.

6. Let it cool and then remove.

Nutritional info per serving

Calories 119; carbs: 1.6g; fats: 11g; protein: 3g

Deli Meringue Cookies

Whip up these almost zero carb cookies when craving something sweet and keeping your daily macros in check.

Prep Time: 10minutes

Cook Time: 50minutes

Servings: 18

Ingredients

4 large egg whites

½ teaspoon of almond extract

¼ teaspoon cream of tartar

6 tablespoons of Swerve Confectioners

Pinch of salt

Preparation

1. Preheat oven to 210°F.

2. Combine egg whites and cream of tartar in a mixing bowl of your mixer and mix slowly at first and at medium speed.

3. Once frothy, stop mixing and add 3 tablespoons of Swerve, almond extract, and salt. Now set mixer on high speed until the egg whites are whipped up. Stop mixing, add another 3 tablespoons of Swerve and continue to whip on high until it becomes very stiff.

4. Stop mixing and scrape out the meringue from the whisk and the sides of the bowl and mix one more time to ensure an even mix.

5. Transfer the meringue into a piping bag. If using a smaller bag, fill a couple of times until batch is exhausted.

6. Line 2 or 3 baking sheets with parchment paper and pipe out your desired shapes numbering 18, (I use rosette).

7. Bake the cookies 40-50 minutes at 210°F. Meringue cookies are done when they can be peeled easily from parchment paper without sticking. Leave to cool 30 minutes before removing.

Nutritional info per serving

Calories 4.11; carbs: 0g; fats: 0.9g; protein: 0.8g

Simple Vanilla Ice Cream

Prep Time: 15minutes

Freeze Time: 2-4 hours

Servings: 4-5

Ingredients

2 cups of canned coconut milk, full-fat

1/3 cup xylitol sweetener

1/8 teaspoon of salt

1 1/2 teaspoon of vanilla bean paste

Preparation

1. Combine milk, vanilla, sweetener, salt, stirring well.

2. Churn mixture in an ice cream maker according to the manufacturer's instructions.

3. Alternatively, freeze in ice cube trays and then blend frozen mixture in a high-speed blender.

Nutritional Info per serving

Calories 184; carbs: 4.04g; fats: 19g; protein: 1.8g

Fatty Vanilla Ice Cream

Enjoy this not so simple but delicious and fat-packed vanilla ice cream.

Prep Time: 5minutes

Cook Time: 15 minutes

Servings: 2

Ingredients

2 eggs, yolks& whites

1¼ cups of heavy whipping cream

½ teaspoon of vanilla extract

2 tablespoons of erythritol (optional)

Preparation

1. Separate eggs. Whisk the egg yolks in a bowl until smooth. Set the egg whites aside.

2. Add together the cream, vanilla and sweetener in a pan. Bring mixture to boil and let it simmer 2-3 minutes until it thickens a little.

3. Lower heat and pour the egg yolks into the mixture of hot cream. Simmer on low heat with frequent stirring until thicken

4. Place to cool in the refrigerator.

5. Beat the reversed egg whites until fluffy and then fold into the cream mixture.

6. Churn in an ice cream maker following manufacturer's instructions or place in a jar, cover and freeze with occasional stir until desired consistency is attained.

Nutritional Info per serving

Calories 581; carbs: 5g; fats: 58g; protein: 11g

Raspberry Ice Cream

So bright, so creamy and so tasty!

Prep Time: 60minutes

Freeze Time: 4 hours

Servings: 16

Yield: ½ cup

Ingredients

24 oz of raspberries, frozen

5 oz allulose

2 oz of fromage blanc

8 ounce of heavy whipping cream

Preparation

1. Thaw raspberries for about 45 minutes.

2. In a bowl, add together the heavy whipping cream and the fromage blanc.

3. Once raspberries are thawed, puree in a blender, strain and discard seeds.

4. Add in the allulose and stir to mix and dissolve.

5. Pour in the raspberry mixture to the cream mixture and mix well.

6. Refrigerate 4-6 hours.

7. Use an ice cream maker to churn out, following the manufacturer's instructions.

Nutritional Info per serving

Calories 73.16; carbs: 4.04g; fats: 5.42g; protein: 1.12g

Raspberry Yoghurt Ice Cream

A mouthwatering variation you'll want to try.

Prep Time: 60minutes

Coo Freeze Time: 4 hours

Servings: 16

Yield: ½ cup

Ingredients

24 oz of raspberries, frozen

7 oz erythritol

2 oz of Greek or mascarpone yogurt

8-10 drops of liquid stevia

8 ounce of heavy whipping cream

Preparation

1. Thaw raspberries for about 45 minutes.

2. In a bowl, add together the heavy whipping cream and the yoghurt.

3. Once raspberries are thawed, puree in a blender, strain and discard seeds.

4. Add in the erythritol and stir to mix and dissolve.

5. Pour in the raspberry mixture to the cream mixture and mix well.

6. Refrigerate 4-6 hours.

7. Use an ice cream maker to churn out, following the manufacturer's instructions.

Nutritional Info per serving

Calories 73.16; carbs: 4.04g; fats: 5.42g; protein: 1.12g

Chocolate Ice Cream

The dessert to love!

Prep Time: 5 minutes

Cook Time: 0 minutes

Servings: 2

Ingredients:

1 can of coconut milk

1 teaspoon of chocolate stevia

2 tablespoons of unsweetened cocoa powder

A pinch of salt

Preparation

1. Combine all the ingredients in a blender.

2. Pour the chocolate mixture into an ice cream machine and follow the direction of the manufacturer. *Serve!*

Nutritional Info Per Serving

Calories - 318, Carbs – 9.1g, Fat – 28.6g, Proteins – 3g

Lemon Ice Cream

A lusciously citrus-flavored dessert for the whole family.

Prep Time: 15 minutes

Cook Time: 0 minutes

Servings: 2

Ingredients:

1 lemon or lime, juice and zest

3 eggs

1¾ cups heavy whipping cream

1/3 cup erythritol

¼ tsp yellow food coloring (optional)

Preparation

1. Begin by washing the lemon and then the outer peel for the zest and squeeze out the juice as well.

2. Separate eggs. In a bowl, beat the egg whites until it is stiff. In a different bowl, whisk the egg yolks and erythritol until fluffy.

3. Add the lemon juice and if using, yellow food coloring. Fold the egg whites gently into the yolk mixture. Carefully fold egg whites into yolk mixture.

4. In a bowl, whip the cream until soft peaks are formed and then fold the egg mixture into the cream.

5. Use an ice cream maker to freeze as directed by the manufacturer. Alternatively place bowl in the freezer and stir every 30 minutes for 2 hours or so until desired consistency is attained.

Nutritional info per serving

Calories 269; carbs: 3g; fats: 27g; protein: 7g

3-ingredient No Churn Ice Cream

Satisfy your sweet tooth with this easy ice cream recipe.

Prep Time: 5 minutes

Freeze Time: 4 hours

Servings: 4

Ingredients:

2 cups heavy whipping cream, divided

4 tablespoons of monk fruit sweetener, divided

1 1/2 teaspoon of pure vanilla extract, divided

Preparation

1. Combine ingredients in a 2 mason jars.

2. Shake well for 5 minutes and then place in the freezer to freeze until solid, shaking the jars every hour or so.

3. Enjoy chilled!

Nutritional info per serving

Calories 400; carbs: 3.91g; fats: 44g; protein: 2.45g

Creamy Keto Ice Cream

Prep Time: 10 minutes

Freeze Time: 4 hours

Servings: 5

Ingredients:

1/2 cup of unsweetened plain almond milk

1 1/2 cups of heavy whipping cream

1/2 cup of confectioners swerve sweetener

1 1/2 teaspoons vanilla extract

Preparation

1. Combine all the ingredients in a bowl, whisking the sweetener until fully dissolved.

2. Place in the freezer and freeze until the edges of the mixture starts to set. Scrape down sides and beat with a hand mixer on low for 30 seconds until smooth. Place back in the freezer.

3. 30 minutes later, repeat this process until the mixture becomes firm when beaten for the last time, then use a spatula to flatten the surface of the ice cream.

4. Cover and place back in the freezer until the ice cream is frozen.

5. Before serving, thaw a bit and enjoy!

Nutritional info per serving

Calories 250; carbs: 2g; fats: 26g; protein: 2g

Almond Chocolate Smoothie

enjoy your chocolate, without making excuses.

Prep Time: 5 minutes

Cook Time: 0 minutes

Servings: 1

Ingredients:

8 raw almonds

1 cup of unsweetened almond milk

3 ice cubes

1/2 scoop of chocolate protein powder

Preparation

Blend ingredients in a blender until smooth.

Nutrition Info Per Serving

Calories: 153, Fat: 7.7g, Carbs: 6.2g, Protein: 15.6g

Coconut Strawberry Milkshake

Prep Time: 3 minutes

Cook Time: 0 minutes

Servings: 2

Ingredients:

2 cups of coconut milk, full fat

1 cup of strawberries

¼ cup of cacao powder

2 scoops vanilla protein powder

7 ice cubes

Preparation

1. Blend all the ingredients, except the ice cubes, in a Vitamix or any other high powered blender for a minute.

2. For about 30 seconds, add the ice cubes one after the other, and keep blending until smooth.

Nutritional Info Per Serving:

Calories - 685, Carbs: 17.8g, Fat: 60.4g, Proteins: 28g

CUSTARDS, PUDDINGS & MOUSSE

Caramel Creme Brulee

Enjoy this rich custard-based dessert

Prep Time: 30 minutes

Cook Time: 45 minutes

Servings: 2

Ingredients

1 teaspoon butter

¾ cup erythritol

½ cup heavy cream

1 teaspoon of vanilla

2 egg yolks

Preparation

1. To make the caramel, place 1/3 of the erythritol in a deep pot and heat, with frequent stirring, on medium heat.

2. Add 1/8 cup of water and stir. Once it begins to froth and rise, add the butter and once the color turns darker, remove from heat. Spoon evenly into ramekins and wait for it to harden.

3. Next, make the crème brulee by mixing 1/3 of erythritol and the egg yolks in a bowl.

4. Get a separate bowl and mix together the vanilla and heavy cream. And then whisk gently into the egg yolks.

5. Pour this mixture into the hardened caramel in the ramekins and place in a pan or a casserole dish. Fill the outer pan or dish with boiling water, ensuring that it doesn't splash into the ramekins.

6. Bake 45 minutes at 350F until firm on the outside. Let it cool and then ladle the rest of the erythritol onto the custard.

7. Caramelize the sugar substitute with a broiler. Cool, harden, and enjoy!

Nutritional info per serving

Calories 314; carbs: 2.57g; fats: 31.74g; protein: 4.45g

Lemony Cheesecake Mousse

For those times when your body really needs a treat!

Prep Time: 10 minutes

Cook Time: 0 minutes

Servings: 5

Ingredients:

8 oz of cream cheese or mascarpone cheese

1 cup of heavy cream

1/4 cup of lemon juice

1 cup heavy cream

½ to1 teaspoon of lemon liquid stevia

1/8 teaspoon of salt

Preparation

1. Add the cheese and lemon juice in a mixer and blend until smooth.

2. Add the remaining ingredients and then blend well together until whipped.

3. If you like, adjust sweetener.

4. Keep refrigerated until it is time to serve.

Nutritional Info Per Serving

Calories - 277, Carbs - 1.7g, Fat - 29.6g, Proteins - 3.7g,

Dairy-Free Chocolate Pudding

A delicious pudding that is also dairy-free.

Prep Time: 10 minutes

Cook Time: 2 minutes

Servings: 2

Ingredients:

1 tablespoon of dark cocoa powder

2 tablespoons of sweetener

1 cup of unsweetened coconut milk

1/2 teaspoon of glucomannan powder

Preparation

1. In a bowl that's microwaveable, pour the coconut milk, the cocoa powder and sweetener. Whisk the mixture thoroughly to blend well.

2. While still whisking, sprinkle the glucomannan powder bit by bit over it. Whisk thoroughly to take out the lumps.

3. Heat the bowl in a microwave for 1 minute 30 seconds or until it is heated but not boiling.

4. Remove the bowl and give a final whisk.

5. Cover the bowl and refrigerate for several hours or until the mixture thickens and cools completely.

Nutritional Info Per Serving

Calories - 81, Carbs -3.3g, Fat - 6.5g, Proteins - 2.1g

Chocolate Gelatin Pudding

Gelatin works wonder! It heals the gut lining and improves the skin, hair and nails. Since it is packed with collagen, it aids detoxification and reduces wrinkles.

Prep Time: 10minutes

Cook Time: 5minutes

Servings: 2

Ingredients

1 cup coconut milk (canned, full fat)

2 tablespoons of organic cocoa or cacao powder

1/2 teaspoon stevia powder extract

1 tablespoon of quality gelatin

2 tablespoon of water

Preparation

1. Combine the cocoa, coconut milk and sweetener in a pot and heat while stirring over medium heat.

2. In a small bowl, combine the gelatin water thoroughly and then add to the pan, stirring until dissolved.

3. Once warm, transfer into ramekins and refrigerate for 30 to 45 minutes.

4. Serve and enjoy!

Nutritional info per serving

Calories 84; carbs: 8g; fats: 5g; protein: 2g

Lemon Semi-Frozen Dessert

A sugar-free semifreddo dessert with great taste!

Prep Time: 25minutes

Freeze Time: 8 hours

Servings: 8

Ingredients:

3/4 cup of xylitol, divided

1/4 cup lemon juice

8 egg yolks

2 tablespoons of vodka

1 cup whipping cream

1/8 teaspoon salt

Preparation

1. Combine ½ of the xylitol, lemon juice, egg yolks, vodka and salt in a double boiler and whisk until thick and doubled in volume. Let the mixture cool completely on a bowl of ice water.

2. Combine the remaining xylitol that's left and the whipping cream in a bowl and then whisk with an electric mixer until firm peaks form.

3. Now fold the cooled custard gently into the whipped cream with a spatula. Spoon onto a greased and plastic-lined loaf pan, fold the wrap over the custard and let it freeze for 8-12 hours until frozen.

4. Unfold wrap, transfer your semi-frozen dessert to a plate and peel the plastic wrap off.

5. Serve and enjoy!

Nutritional info per serving

Calories 180; carbs: 12g; fats: 16g; protein: 3g

Chocolate Semifreddo

Prep Time: 3 minutes

Cook Time: 0 minutes

Servings: 4

Ingredients:

1 cup cream

3 egg yolks

21/2 teaspoon of Truvia

1.4 oz chocolate

Pinch of salt

Preparation

1. Combine all the ingredients except the eggs in a jug and place in a microwave to heat for about 2 minutes or until it almost at boiling point. Use a stick blender to mix well.

2. Now add the egg yolks and mix again with the blender.

3. Return to microwave and let it heat for about a minute with 20 seconds intervals, blending well at each interval.

4. Let it cool and place in ramekins. Freeze for 30 to 60 minutes before serving

Nutritional info per serving

Calories 259; carbs: 6g; fats: 25g; protein: 6g

Keto Chocolate Brownies

A flourless gluten-free low-sugar dessert that taste just like real brownies!

Prep Time: 10 minutes

Cook Time 35 minutes

Servings: 6

Ingredients

1/2 cup of chocolate chips, sugar-free

1/2 cup of butter

3 eggs

1/4 cup keto sweetener of choice

1 teaspoon of vanilla extract

Preparation

1. Add butter and chocolate to a bowl and melt in the microwave for a minute or less. Take it out and stir thoroughly to melt the remaining clumps (do not leave in the microwave until completely melted).

2. Add eggs, vanilla and sweetener to a bowl and blend until frothy.

3. Slowly pour the melted butter and chocolate in the egg mix bowl and whisk to incorporate well.

4. Pour into cake pan and bake for 30 to 35 minutes at 350°F until an inserted knife in the middle comes out clean.

5. Serve as is or with whipped cream, if you like.

Nutritional info per serving

Calories 224; carbs: 3g; fats: 23g; protein: 4g

Almond Fudge Brownies

Prep Time: 5minutes

Cook Time: 11minutes

Servings: 16

Ingredients

1 cup of almond butter

3 large eggs

3/4 cup powdered of erythritol

10 tablespoons of unsweetened cocoa powder

1/2 teaspoon of baking powder

Preparation

1. Add the almond butter and the erythritol to a food processor and blend together.

2. Add the eggs, baking powder, cocoa powder and a pinch of salt.

3. Next, remove the batter to a greased baking pan and make it smooth by using a spatula.

4. Bake at 325°F for 11 minutes. Cool before cutting.

Nutritional info per serving

Calories 118; carbs: 5g; fats: 11g; protein: 5g

Pumpkin Spice Muffins

These yummy muffins are worth several tries!

Prep Time: 15 minutes

Cook Time: 40 minutes

Servings: 6

Ingredients:

1½ cup of almond flour

2/3 cup of organic pumpkin

2/3 cup of erythritol crystals

4 very large eggs

1 tablespoon of pumpkin pie spice

Preparation

1. Preheat oven to 300°F and use paper liners to line a muffin tin.

2. Thoroughly mix the flour with the erythritol and pumpkin pie spice until it has no lumps.

3. Add the eggs and pumpkin to the bowl. Use an electric mixer to beat the mixture until smooth.

4. Transfer the mixture to the muffin tin and bake for 30-40 minutes or until a stick inserted in the muffins center comes out almost clean.

5. Remove from oven and cover the tin with a towel to cool.

Nutritional Information Per Serving

Calories - 224, Carbs – 4.4g, Fat – 17.7g, Proteins – 11.3g

Dill Pickle Dip
Very flavorful and easy to make!

Prep Time: 5minutes

Cook Time: minutes

Servings: 12 cookies

Yields: 11/2 cups

Ingredients

12 ounce cream cheese, softened

6 tablespoons of pickle juice

1/3 cup dill pickle, finely chopped

1 tablespoon of fresh dill, chopped

Preparation

1. Add the pickle juice gradually to the softened cream cheese until desired consistency is attained.

2. Add the pickle and fresh dill and then stir well to mix.

3. Chill 30 minutes and then serve.

Nutritional info per serving

Calories 99; carbs: 1g; fats: 9g; protein: 1g

Cheesy Pizza Dip

A crust-less pizza dip with lots of goodness!

Prep Time: 5minutes

Cook Time: 25minutes

Servings: 12

Yields: 1- 9-inch pie

Ingredients

8 oz brick-style cream cheese, softened

1 1/2 cups of mozzarella cheese, grated, divided

1 cup of parmesan cheese, finely grated, divided

1 cup of marinara or red sauce

15 pepperoni slices

Preparation

1. Preheat oven to 375°F.

2. Spread the cream cheese evenly over the bottom of a greased9-inch pie dish and then sprinkle ¾ cup of mozzarella cheese over it.

3. Next, sprinkle half cup of the parmesan and add the marinara or red sauce evenly to cover the cheese.

4. Sprinkle over ¾ mozzarella evenly and ½ cup parmesan evenly and then top the cheeses with pepperoni slices.

5. Bake about 25 minutes or until cheeses melted. Let it cool and then serve.

Nutritional info per serving

Calories 151; carbs: 4g; fats: 12g; protein: 7g

Chocolate Almond Balls

A simple and tasty vegan bite recipe that even kids will love.

Prep Time: 5minutes

Cook Time: 5minutes

Servings: 12

Ingredients

1/2 cup of almond flour

1/2 cup of almond butter

1/2 teaspoon of vanilla extract

1/2 cup vegan chocolate chips

2 tablespoons almonds, chopped

Preparation

1. In a bowl, add together the flour, butter and vanilla extract together. Mix well to combine.

2. Shape the now soft dough into balls of ½ inches and place on lined baking sheet. Freeze 20 minutes.

3. Melt the chocolate chips in a microwave, with frequent stirring, for 2 minutes.

4. Dip the balls into the melted chocolate and place on the baking sheet. Sprinkle the chopped almond over and set aside for 10 minutes to set.

Nutritional info per serving

Calories 102; carbs: 3,5g; fats: 9.2g; protein: 2.9g

FAT BOMBS

Simple Chocolate Fat Bombs

This should do when you crave a quick treat.

Prep Time: 5 minutes

Cook Time: 0 minutes

Servings: 8

Ingredients:

1/4 cup of coconut oil

1/4 cup of cocoa butter

10 drops of vanilla stevia drops

Preparation

1. In a double boiler or microwave, melt the coconut oil and cocoa butter over low heat.

2. Take out from heat, add the stevia and stir to combine.

3. Pour the mixture into molds and refrigerate molds until solid.

Nutritional info per serving

Calories 125; carbs: 0g; fats: 10g; protein: 0g

Choco Peanut Butter Fat Bombs

Pop these in whenever the sugar craving come calling or feeling hungry in between meals.

Prep Time: 1minute

Cook Time: 10minutes

Servings: 12

Ingredients

¼ cup of virgin coconut oil

¼ cup peanut butter

3 tablespoons unsweetened cocoa powder

2-4 tablespoons stevia

Splash of vanilla extract (optional)

Preparation

1. Melt the peanut butter and coconut oil. Add the cocoa powder, stevia and stir.

2. Remove from heat and then if using, add vanilla extract.

3. Pour into silicone molds and freeze until set.

4. Remove from molds, place in a container and refrigerate.

Nutritional info per serving

Calories 88; carbs: 2.2g; fats: 8.7g; protein: 1.7g

Nutty Berry Fat Bombs

Satiate your sweet tooth cravings.

Prep time: 25 minutes

Cook time: 10 minutes

Servings: 12

Ingredients:

1/2 cup of coconut, unsweetened, shredded

1/2 cup of dried raspberries, frozen

1/2 cup of coconut butter

1/2 cup of coconut oil

1/4 cup of powdered Swerve Sweetener

Preparation

1. Use parchment paper to line a baking pan, preferably an 8 x 8.

2. Use a food processor or coffee grinder to pulse the raspberries into fine powder and then keep aside.

3. In a medium saucepan, mix the shredded coconut, butter, swerve and coconut oil, cooking over medium heat and stirring often until the ingredients melts and are thoroughly mixed.

4. Put half of the coconut mix into the baking pan and then add the ground raspberries to the mixture that's in the pan. Stir well until thoroughly mixed.

5. Fold the ground raspberry mix over the top of the coconut mix in the saucepan. Use a knife to swirl it together.

6. To set, refrigerate or freeze. Afterwards, break into chunks.

Nutritional info per serving

Calories 234; carbs: 6.56g; fats: 23.56g; protein: 1.7g

Strawberry Fat Bomb

Keto Strawberry Fat Bomb

Load up fats on your body— in a healthy way!

Prep time: 10 minutes

Cook time: 0 minutes

Servings: 12

Ingredients:

2 cups of heavy cream, organic

1 tablespoon of strawberry sweetener

2 to 4 tablespoons swerve

1 teaspoon of strawberry extract, optional

Preparation

1. In a bowl, add cream and whip until it forms peaks. Add the remaining ingredients and thoroughly mix.

2. Scoop 2 tablespoons of this mixture onto a baking pan that's been lined with parchment paper.

3. Freeze for about 30 minutes until hardened.

Nutritional info per serving

Calories 133; carbs: 0g; fats: 16g; protein: 0g

Coconut & Ginger Fat Bombs

It's simply yum!

Prep time: 5 minutes

Cook time: 0 minutes

Servings: 10

Ingredients:

3 ounces of coconut oil, softened

3 ounces of coconut butter, softened

1 teaspoon of ginger powder

1/4 cup of unsweetened desiccated/shredded coconut

1 teaspoon of granulated sweetener

Preparation

1. Whisk all the ingredients together in a large bowl until the sweetener dissolves.

2. Pour the mixture into ice cube trays or silicone molds and refrigerate for at least 10 minutes.

Nutritional info per serving

Calories 120; carbs: 2.2g; fats: 12.8g; protein: 0.5g

Dark Macadamia Fat Bombs
Mouthwatering and delightful!

Prep time: 10 minutes

Cook time: 0 minutes

Servings: 6

Ingredients:

4 ounces chopped macadamias

2 ounces of cocoa butter

¼ cup of heavy cream or coconut oil

2 tablespoons of cocoa powder, unsweetened

2 tablespoons of swerve

Preparation

1. In a small pan or microwave, melt the butter and then add the cocoa powder.

2. Add the swerve as well; combine thoroughly until it's all melted and well-mixed.

3. Stir in the macadamia nuts.

4. Add the cream or coconut oil; combine and give it time to return to temperature.

5. Pour the mixture into paper candy cups or molds; cool for a while.

6. Refrigerate until firm.

Nutritional info per serving

Calories 267; carbs: 3g; fats: 28g; protein: 3g

Berry Cheesecake Fat Bombs

Prep time: 10 minutes

Cook time: 0 minutes

Servings: 6

Ingredients:

6 Strawberries

1 cup cream cheese

1/4 cup of berries

3 tablespoons of water

Preparation

1. Combine the strawberries, cream cheese and a tablespoon of water in a blender and blend mixture until smooth.

2. Transfer to a silicon ice cube tray and then freeze for 10 minutes.

3. Blend the rest of the ingredients and pour over the half frozen mixture in the ice cube tray.

4. Freeze and enjoy anytime!

Nutritional info per serving

Calories 125; carbs: 3g; fats: 12g; protein: 3g

Cheesecake Keto Fat Bomb

An ice-cream-like treat to indulge in!

Prep time: 10 minutes

Cook time: 0 minutes

Servings: 18

Ingredients:

6 oz cream cheese, softened

2 - 2.5 oz raspberries or strawberries, softened

4 tablespoons of salted butter, softened

2 tablespoons granular swerve sweetener

1 teaspoon vanilla extract

Preparation

1. Blend the strawberries in a blender or by hand.

2. Add together the pureed strawberries together with the vanilla and sweetener in a bowl, stirring well to mix.

3. Place the cream cheese in a microwave to soften for 10 seconds or thereabout and then add it to the bowl. Add the butter as well and mix with an electric mixer to remove clumps.

4. Divide batter into silicone molds and use a spatula to smoothen the surface. Freeze until solid.

Nutritional info per serving

Calories 60; carbs: 0.5g; fats: 6g; protein: 1g

Ginger Coconut Fat Bombs

Add a pleasant zing to your fat bomb with this recipe

Prep time: 3 minutes

Cook time: 0 minutes

Servings: 10

Ingredients:

1/3 cup coconut butter softened

1/3 cup coconut oil softened

¼ cup desiccated/shredded coconut unsweetened

1 tsp granulated sweetener

1 tsp ginger powder

Preparation

1. Combine all the ingredients in a jug and mix well.

2. Pour into ice block trays and silicon molds and freeze for at least 10 minutes.

Nutritional info per serving

Calories120; carbs: 2.2 g; fats: 12.8 g; protein: 0.5g

Sugar-free Caramel Sauce

Prep Time: 0 minutes

Cook Time: 10 minutes

Servings: 1

Ingredients

1/3 cup of salted butter

3 tbsp granulated sweetener

2/3 cup heavy cream

1 teaspoon of vanilla extract

Preparation

1. In a saucepan, melt butter and granulated sweetener over low heat. Cook and stir melted butter and sweetener for about 4 minutes, stirring often, until golden brown. Do not let it burn.

2. Add the cream and let it boil. Lower the heat to let it simmer for about 10minutes, but no more. Keep stirring until it becomes thick and of a caramel color.

3. Remove from heat and add the vanilla extract, whisking well.

4. Let it cool so as to thicken.

Nutritional info per serving

Calories 91; carbs: 0g; fats: 9 g; protein: 0g

Cream Cheese Pancakes

Prep Time: 2minutes

Cook Time: 15minutes

Servings: 2

Yield: 6 small pancakes

Ingredients

4 oz cream cheese

2 large eggs

1/4 cup of almond flour

1/2 teaspoon of baking powder

1/4 teaspoon of salt

Cooking spray, for greasing pan

Preparation

1. In a blender, blend together the eggs, cream cheese, baking flour, flour and salt until smooth.

2. In a heated coated pan, pour in 3 tablespoons of the batter and cook about 3 minutes until the pancake is golden brown. Flip and cook another 1-2 minutes until the other side is golden brown as well.

3. Transfer to a plate and repeat process with the rest of the batter.

4. Enjoy, with sliced strawberries or monk fruit, if desired.

5. Store leftover tightly in a container and refrigerate for up to 4 days.

Nutritional info per serving

Calories 329; carbs: 5.4g; fats: 30.2g; protein: 10.1g

Lemon Almond Tart/ Pie Crust

Make the perfect shortbread crust for a lemon meringue pie or a summer fruit tart.

Prep Time: 10minutes

Cook Time: 15minutes

Servings: 1

Ingredients

6 tablespoons of butter

2 cups of almond flour

1/3 cup granulated sweetener

1 teaspoon of lemon zest, freshly grated

Preparation

1. Melt butter and then add the almond flour, lemon zest and sweetener, mixing well to combine until crumbly.

2. Press the dough into tart or into pie tins.

3. Finally, bake at 350°F in a preheated oven for 15 minutes until golden brown and firm.

Nutritional info per serving for1/8th tart crust

Calories 238; carbs: 3g; fats: 23g; protein: 6g

Coconut Cream With Berries

Dairy-free whipped cream with berries

Prep Time: 5 minutes

Cook Time 3 minutes

Servings: 2

Ingredients

1 Can of unsweetened full fat coconut milk

Berries of choice

Dash of vanilla extract (optional)

Dark chocolate (optional)

Preparation

1. Refrigerate coconut milk for 12 to 24 hours.

2. Scoop the thick part of the coconut milk out but leave behind the water.

3. Use a hand mixer to whip for 2 to 3 minutes.

4. Add the berries, mixing well.

5. Add the vanilla, if using and top with the chocolate shaving. *Yummy!*

Nutritional info per serving

Calories 249; carbs: 11g; fats: 24 g; protein: 0g

Sugar-free Lemon Curd

Prep Time: 5 minutes

Cook Time: 10 minutes

Servings: 1 cup

Ingredients

1/2 cup of lemon juice, Meyer preferably

2 tablespoons + 2 teaspoons of Truvia

2 large egg yolks

2 large eggs

6 tablespoons of butter, cubed

Preparation

1. In a saucepan, whisk the eggs, egg yolks, sweetener and lemon juice together.

2. Add the butter, and heat on medium or low heat, stirring often. (Too much heat isn't good for the egg in the mixture). Increase heat when butter is completely melted.

3. Stir to thicken and then remove.

4. Now pass through a strainer to remove any bits of egg. Refrigerate.

Nutritional info per serving

Calories 890; carbs: 10g; fats: 88 g; protein: 19g

Whipped Cream

Contains neither dairy nor sugar.

Preparation time: 10 minutes

Cooking time: 0 minutes

Servings: 8

Ingredients:

2 drops of full vanilla liquid stevia

1 can of full fat coconut milk, cream only

Directions:

1. Beat the ingredients in a stand mixer on speed 4 until it thickens.

2. Store in the refrigerator.

Nutritional Information Per Serving

Calories - 34, Carbohydrates – 0.6g, Fat – 3.1g, Proteins – 0.3g, Fiber – 0g

Keto Coconut Slice

3 ingredients, 5 minutes and you can have the best keto dessert!

Prep Time: 5 minutes

Cook Time 0 minutes

Servings:

Ingredients

2 cups coconut unsweetened, desiccated

1/2 cup salted butter, melted

1/4 cup of erythritol

Preparation

1. Add the desiccated coconut to a mixing bowl.

2. In a microwave, melt the butter and add the erythritol, stirring well to mix.

3. Line a baking tin with parchment paper and pour the mixture into it. Press firmly down to level the top.

4. Freeze 1 hour and then enjoy!

Nutritional info per serving

Calories 266; carbs: 1.8g; fats: 27.5 g; protein: 1.8g

Chocolate Frosty

Prep Time: 0 minutes

Cook Time: 10 minutes

Servings: 3

Ingredients

1 cup of heavy whipping cream

1 tablespoon of almond butter

2 tablespoons of unsweetened cocoa powder

1 teaspoon vanilla extract

5 drops of liquid stevia

Preparation

1. Beat heavy cream with a hand mixer for 2-3 minutes in a bowl.

2. Add the remaining ingredients and blend to thicken.

3. Freeze for about 30 minutes to desired consistency. *Enjoy*!

Nutritional info per serving

Calories 183; carbs: 4.3g; fats: 18.3 g; protein: 2.7g

The End